CW00918575

A Bird

Called Wisdom

Poems on Grief, Transformation, and Renewal

Dolores Cruz

Printed Worldwide
First Printing 2023
First Edition 2023

10 9 8 7 6 5 4 3 2 1

Edited by Shelby Leigh
Book cover design – Katarina Naskovski
All photos by Dolores Cruz
with the exception of:
Just Here – DrewAnn Andrews
Madrid – Vanessa Cruz
Peace – Vanessa Cruz

A Bird

Called Wisdom

To my family—
my husband Joey, and our four children,
Nicholas, Jessica, Vanessa, and Eric (in spirit),
who strengthen and inspire me each day
with their unconditional love.

Table of Contents

Acknowledgments

I would like to acknowledge the people who have provided consistent support to me on my grief journey, which has brought me to this book I share with you today:

First and foremost, my husband, Joey, and children, Nicholas, Jessica, and Vanessa—That first night of Eric's passing, when all the friends and family had gone home, my husband and children stood in the living room in a huddled embrace of painful confusion. Joey, with heavy grief evident in his voice, assured us, "We have each other, and we will get through this. We *will* get through this." And we have. We have grieved together, and also supported each other while we have grieved individually. Each of my kids have expressed in their own unique ways their unwavering and never-ending love for their beloved baby brother. Because of each of them, Eric's presence is always felt.

That first year, my incredibly gifted grief therapist, Dr. Jennifer Levin, gently carried me on this hardest journey ever. I was heard, I was loved, and in time I found a way to come up for air and stand tall again on my own two feet as a result of her astute guidance. I am forever grateful.

Two support groups were instrumental in my life-long process of healing. Helping Parents Heal, directed by lead admin Elizabeth Boisson, is an international organization for parents whose child has passed away. Finding this group was lifesaving for me. Additionally, through groups led by grief specialist

David Kessler, I have found other communities that gently hold space while witnessing each other's pain. I am honored to be able to give back as a leader/moderator of these in-person and online groups.

So many friends and other family members made themselves consistently available to me and my immediate family to talk with, too many to name. This support was immensely helpful when I didn't think I could keep living. I only hope I can do the same in return when needed.

And of course, I am hugely grateful to my editor, Shelby Leigh, who guided me with expertise and unending patience while I painstakingly and lovingly crafted this book.

This life is a beautiful, magnificent adventure as well as an awful, agonizing ordeal. It's not either/or; it is both. That's the reality. We can't have the amazing and awesome without the painful and the terrible. And we are here to hold each other up, listen to each other's stories, and offer as much love as our hearts can give. This is our purpose on this Earth—to take care of each other in the challenges and celebrate with each other in the joys.

Preface

It never occurred to me to be a poet. I never planned to be a poet. But in retrospect, the words were always there, deep inside, and during the most poignant moments of my life—the greatest joys and most challenging tribulations—those words fell out onto the paper. Other than those occasional opportunities, they stayed tucked neatly inside my heart.

Until May of 2017 when every parent's worst nightmare became my reality. My youngest of four children, my son, Eric, was killed in a car accident. I was catapulted into the deepest grief I had ever experienced. I grappled for some kind of hold on life, which now held no meaning or purpose whatsoever. I had no idea how to go on.

I began to journal. All my emotions needed to go somewhere, and bottling everything up inside was not an option. As I wrote about my deep pain, my despair, and my anger, I noticed that much of the words came out as poetry. There was no intention to this. It was merely the way the anguish flowed out. It was the river of grief which was unstoppable, unrestrainable. These written words helped me cope with the unimaginable agony of losing a child.

Eventually I came to realize that this expression of poetry saved me. At this point in time, 6 years later, I read these journals and am amazed at the journey I took, and still take, of healing my heart and my soul through expression. I now share them with you in the hopes that my words may resonate with you, may touch a place in you that has suffered and endured.

I have learned that it's possible for
grief and joy to co-exist.

PART 1

THE FALL

Shattered

At the break of dawn
I rise and look for you
A foreboding
An empty bed
An unanswered text
A discomfort in my pounding heart
Your sister's sleepy, frightened eyes
As I anxiously exhale the words
Have you heard from Eric?
In that moment
A gut-wrenching pound on the door
The sound of our footsteps down the stairs
Something inside of me knew
What was on the other side of that door
I dreaded opening it
But there was no turning back
A coroner
A sheriff
The words "Eric" and "passed away" in the same sentence
Our knees buckled
Our shrieks splattered against the walls
We doubled over
And began the fall into the abyss
This was not possible
Not possible
Not possible…

These Flowers

Who are these flowers for?
Why are these people here?
A house filled with pain
And horrified, grief-stricken faces.
Guests at the door
Holding casseroles and bottled waters
Pastries and lattes
And flowers.
All burning with the unimaginable news
That your handsome face
Is no more.
Tears
Disbelief
Stories of your acts of compassion
Your words of kindness
Your loyal friendship.
We don't know how we ended up here
For this.
Surreal.
We are floating through it all.
Can we please go back 24 hours
So we can laugh with you again?

Abyss

You left
And I have fallen
Into an abyss
Deep and dark
Nothing above
Or below
Nothing left
Or right
It is black
It is bleak
No light
No air
And no way out.

Burial

It's the day after the burial.

Burial…

Can hardly even say it.
Quiet house.
So many had been here,
but it's silent now.

Reflection
and more pain.
What do we do with it?
Where do we put it?
Confusion,
anger,
incomprehension,
a blur,
a blunder,
a folly.
It should not be.
How to live with something
that *should not be?*

You,
my Eric.
So great,
so large,
so full of life,

so full of love.
Your love exploded out into the world
every single day—
felt by hundreds,
thousands.

We all need you here.
We all want you here.
We are empty
and no longer know how to make any sense
of this ridiculous life.

Right Here

God,
I am right here.
I have always been
right here.
Always loving you.
Always ready to serve you.

I want to know
I want to know
I want to know

WHY AM I HERE?
WHAT IS THE POINT?
WHAT IS IT YOU WANT ME TO DO?
WHY DID IT HAPPEN?

Why won't you tell me?

Can anyone please explain it to me?
Anyone?
Anyone?

I want to know
I want to know

My son
I need you near.
I need to know you are here.

Walk with me.
Hug me.
Take care of me.
Take care of all of us.

You left
and everything fell apart.
I am lost.
I don't know what to do.
All I can do
is keep loving you.

No Photos

Don't show me those photos, please.
They cause me too much pain.
Don't play me his music, please.
I don't want to be reminded.
The ache in my heart is unbearable.

I will protect myself
with denial
of his absence.
Don't talk about it.

I am a shell—
speaking to people
but dead inside.

Not Strong

People say I am strong.

No, I'm not.

They haven't seen me in my car
wailing at the top of my lungs
as I drive home from work.

They haven't seen me hunched over
as I sit on my son's bed
sobbing so uncontrollably
that it's hard to get a breath.

They haven't seen my hands shake so much
that it's almost impossible for me to write.

They haven't noticed that I no longer wear makeup
for I would cry it all off within the hour.

They only see me when I have pulled myself together
and quietly gathered up the broken pieces.

They only see me when I have found a way
to speak in a calm tone,
allowing one word to follow the other,
maybe even finding a way
to shape a smile onto my face.
They see this and say I am strong.

No, I'm not.

For a Moment

I wake up
and for a moment
there is peace.
Could stay there forever
just imagining
you're still in the next room.

Then the reality hits...

Your face,
all those images in my head.
So handsome,
too handsome to be gone.

We all need you here.
Too many are in pain.
How is that right?

It's not right that so many should suffer.
We all need you here.
You were such a blessing and joy to us.

Purpose

We miss you, Son.
We live our lives
but they feel plastic—
like Barbie dolls
and action figures
with fixed eyes
and lifeless smiles—
not full and rich
as they used to be.

Purpose,
purpose—
we seek it.
Why does it seem
to have flown away
with you?

Another Day

Today
I woke up
brushed my teeth
put on my jeans
and my most comfortable t-shirt
kissed my husband
fed the dogs
watered the flowers
stared at the clouds
swallowed some toast
and stood in front of his bedroom door
for 5 minutes.

Then got into the car
with my husband
and drove
someplace I'd never been before.

My husband and I picked out a marker
for our son's grave.

That's not something you do every day.

Just another day
in the life
of a mother
whose youngest child
is missing.

13 Days

So much pain.
It hurts my heart and my stomach.
Don't want to live without you.
Can't imagine how.

You were so perfect.
You were everything to me
to your dad
your sibs
and your sweet girlfriend.
How can we go on?

We look for you,
long to touch you and hug you,
kiss your cheek,
feel your touch.
Such agony without you.

You did everything right—
even your mistakes were right—
because you learned from them
and moved on.

You were in the midst of life,
doing so much at 24.
How could this be?

Who have I been praying to all these years?

What is this life?

I don't get it.
No more joy.
The joy is gone.

Only pain.

Prayer (from Look Around)

In the past,
I always thanked God for my blessings,
and then went on with a list of requests
for blessing others,
which included keeping my loved ones safe,
and helping each of them
with difficulties in their lives.
I even had a list on my nightstand
of people who had lost loved ones
and I included them in my prayers
every night.

But after the Earthly departure
of my son,
those prayers were over.
I was furious,
enraged.
I felt I had been abandoned,
slighted.
After all my years of faithfulness—
then this.

And so my new prayer,
albeit harsh,
fueled by the rawness of my pain,
began:

God,
I want to know who the hell you are.
I want to know who the hell I am.
I want to know what the point of this life is.
I want to know why I'm here.
And I want to know why Eric is not here.

That would be my nightly prayer
for the next many months.

Grief Bursts

I've learned some new terminology.

A grief burst is when
you are going about your day
with the pain of your loss
bubbling underneath the façade of normalcy.

Then suddenly
the anguish bursts through
like the eruption of a geyser
or the explosion of a cannonball.
There is no way to stop it,
your body a helpless vessel
as the sorrow gushes forth.

My therapist says these are also called
love bursts.

I must say,
I have been bursting with love
for quite some time now.

Assumptions

I had a picture in my head
of what life would be like,
a photo in a lovely gold frame.
All my beautiful babies
would grow up and get married
have successful careers and charming children.
My husband and I would grow old
with the love of our children and grandchildren
surrounding us.

But that perfect picture
must have gotten knocked off a high shelf
for it fell and crashed,
shattering into a million pieces.
And like Humpty Dumpty
there is no way to put it back together again.

This assumptive world—
it seems that some of us can have it
and some of us can't.
All I ever wanted was for my family to be intact.

I will never walk you down the aisle.
I will never dance with you at your wedding.
I will never help you move into your new home.
I will never see your kids.

I watch each of my family members crumble.

I watch them suffer.
I hear their anguished cries.
I observe them struggle to get up and take
the next step in their lives.
I watch them choke on their tears.
I watch them wander aimlessly,
stifled, confused.
I am helpless to make it better for them.

What is my purpose?
Why am I here?

Memories of You

I must write them all down
so as not to forget

every look
every smile
every joke
every act of compassion
every nuance

hold them tight
hold them close
don't let them fly away
into the winds of time.

24/7

Because now that you've gone,
left your physical body,
my thoughts are totally obsessed with you,
the one I have lost.

I wash my face.
I think of you.
I crack an egg.
I think of you.
I unlock the car door.
I think of you.
I look up at the clouds as I drive.
I think of you.
I sign in at work.
I think of you.
I open my classroom door.
I think of you.
I help a student with a math problem.
I think of you.
I face the whiteboard to write a sentence.
I think of you.
I listen to the chatter in the lunchroom.
I think of you.
I swallow the sandwich I just chewed.
I think of you.
I stop at a stop sign.
I think of you.
I pet our dog.

I think of you.

I lie underneath the great pine tree
in our front yard,
staring up through her branches
into the beautiful blue sky.
I think of you.
I think of you.
I think of you.
I think of you…

I Dreamed

I dreamed that you and I were in an auditorium with many other people. The joy of being with you again, sitting next to you, flooded my heart. Right there on my left, wearing a button-down shirt. Then we were moved into separate groups. You and I looked across the auditorium, gazing at each other for some moments. This felt like a reflection of what was happening in real life. We are now in separate groups—you on one side of the veil and I on the other—yet still focused on each other.

A Minute Ago

Some days
I can go about my business,
focus on work,
talk to people,
and even laugh with them,
run my errands,
sing with the radio,
and play with my dogs,
all while talking to you
intermittently.
And I think to myself,
"I can do this. I can go on."

I can almost justify your absence
by saying that there is life
and there is death,
we will all die someday,
and I am not the only one
who has lost someone precious.

But then I see a picture of you,
and I look into your eyes,
and I connect with your soul,
and I touch your face in the photo,

and my heart feels heavy,
and I can't believe you're not here.
I feel like you were just here a minute ago.

Wasn't it just a minute ago?

Just Here

84 days

How do I get through this life without you?
You are a part of me,
but you're not here anymore.
There's a hole in me
the size of you.
I'm grasping to pull you back in,
to patch up that hole,
but my fingers grasp the air.

Some days I get by.
Then I slide into what happened—
the what ifs and if onlys.
The grief comes in waves,
smacks me hard
and I go down
into that abyss again,
gasping for air.
Eventually
I breathe.

I see your friends posting
on social media,
making music,
attending concerts,
going out to eat.

You should be with them,
with your girlfriend,
living life to the fullest

like you used to.

When I Close My Eyes

I almost feel

like I can see you

when I

close my eyes,

when I

go to bed

at night,

when I

take a nap,

when I

meditate

in my classroom—

it feels

like

you're here.

Sighting

I saw you
At the birthday party
For your brother-in-law's little niece.

When we first got there
My heart hurt knowing you would have been with us
But then I reminded myself
"He is here."
And left it at that.

We stood outside in the garden area
In a small group
Holding paper plates
Of turkey sandwiches and potato salad
Facing each other
And chatting about things
That mattered so little
Compared to the loudness
of your physical absence.

And then
Without warning
You were there…
To my left
In my peripheral vision
In full color
Hawaiian shirt and blue cap
Your dark scruff

Looking toward the center
Like you were listening in
On the group conversation.

It was just for a few seconds,
Then I very slowly turned my head to the left
To look at you
But your image dissolved
Leaving another party guest standing
where you had been.

I felt peaceful
You were there
Just as I had suspected
And you were just letting me know.

Tattoos

Who knew
I'd ever get one
But if there was ever a time
To do it
It was that night

Your sibs and I
Drove to a tattoo shop
To get them done
Your sister's good friend
Did the art

Nick and Jessica and Vanessa
Got the same one
Your birthday in Roman numerals
On the inside of their forearms

Me
More discreet
A simple heart on the back of my shoulder
With your initials inside
Forever with me

There was magic in that shop
That night
As we honored you
Memorialized you
With ink

I think you were there
Enjoying it all

And over the next few months
Your dad and many of your friends
Did the same

So many bodies
Now permanently displaying
Their love for you

Dream Again

We were walking through a lightly crowded outdoor mall. It was a beautiful day, filled with light. You were on my left, closest to my heart like in the first dream. You wore a button-down shirt and nice pants, the kind you would have worn to work. You still had your closely trimmed facial hair, sparkling eyes—handsome as ever. You hugged your arm around me while we walked and talked. I knew it was a gift to have you with me. We were fine. We were together. All was well.

Party

We had a party for you
four and a half months after you
went to heaven.
No special occasion.
Just needed to bring all your friends
and family together
and play music.
Music.
You were always all about the music.

The band came
and the tunes were loud and joyful,
rocking on,
bringing back all
the most wonderful memories
of you.

And later, many gathered
in the family room
where your drums were,
taking turns on those drums,
each sending strong vibrations
up to the heavens
so you could hear.

We had lots of food and drinks.
The house was full.
All of them here for you.

And they brought something along with them—
love.

The house overflowed with it
just as it had
that first weekend
after you left this world.
There was so much love
I thought the house might lift off its foundation
and float away—

just float away
on love.

When I Reach Out My Hand

When I reach out my hand
do you touch it?
Do you hold it?

If I reach out both hands
will you lift me up
so I may glimpse
the magnificence
the glory
the bliss
the love
of where you are?

New York

New York
Crazy, busy, New York City.

On a short trip for your dad's work
We caught a Broadway show
Which I watched
With new eyes
Because I am not the same person
I used to be

Since you left
It's been hard for me
To be too far away from home
It still is
The longing for you
Intertwined with the longing
For that which comforts me

I miss my home
I miss my bed
I miss my birds
I miss my tree
I miss my patio
I miss my altar

I miss my son
I miss you, my Eric
I'm holding on

Holding on
To seeing you again
When it's my turn to leave this Earth
Seems it will be so long
So long

So I pray
And I learn
And I look for you
And I listen

I think you might've enjoyed the show tonight
So I enjoyed it for you.

Still Around

Your good friend told me about his dream with you. He saw you in the streets of West Hollywood in a coffee shop. You came up to him, but he was sad because he knew that in reality you were gone. You told him to relax and not to mention it to the person he was with. You introduced yourself and asked the person all kinds of questions about himself. (Just like you always did with people you met. Always making them feel important.) And as you talked, your friend was wondering if he could touch you, so he reached out and grabbed your shoulder. He said you looked at him like, "What the heck are you doing?" And then you both started laughing. He said the others must have thought you guys were weirdos. But he knew that the silliness came from his knowing that even though you had left us, here you were with him. How absolutely real that whole dream was. You are letting us all know you still love us, and you are still around.

Thinking...

I am so afraid
for the memories to fade
the wisps of you that I hold on to
but they will indeed dissipate.

Even with the people still here
on this spinning Earth
memories do grow dim.
Even if you had stayed
the pictures in my head
would become fuzzy
or disappear altogether.

I have remembrances
of when all my kids were little
climbing trees
and swinging in swings
looking for worms in the mud
on a rainy day
sweet laughter
and faces as innocent
as cherubs.

Even though I know those days are gone
the memories are treasures
yet the details have floated away
like the steam from hot chocolate.
It's hard to face the aching reality
that there will be no new memories.

Angel

Remember that night
Almost a year ago
A month or two before you left us

It was dusk
There had been an accident on the corner of
That busy intersection
Your sister and I walked down
To see what was going on
I remember the glow of the traffic lights
Red, yellow, and green
Through the dimly lit sky
The white streetlights cascading down
To fill in for the sun's fading light

You came out
Quietly, pensively
To see what was happening
You stood for a bit
Taking it in
I could feel the compassion
Flowing from you

Then
You offered that elderly man—
The one sitting on the curb
Shaken from the accident—
A bottle of water

He took it
He drank it

I was transfixed on this simple act
Of kindness
The world stood still

You were an angel on Earth

More Than a Dream

Your cousin told me that she dreamed of you. It was Christmas and you came in and said hi to her. She said that everyone else disappeared and it was just you and her. She felt shocked, mesmerized. And you were smiling. She mentioned your other cousin, her brother, and you said, "Don't worry about your bro. I'm with him more than he knows." Then she asked you, "What about the rest of us?" And you told her that you're always with us, watching all of us. When she told me that, all time stood still. My breath caught in my throat. I think, just maybe, that it was more than merely a dream.

Conference Thoughts

Eric,
if you came into this room
right now,
it would seem like
I just saw you yesterday…

your face,
your dark hair in place
as always,
your dark eyes
with that mischievous twinkle,
that crooked smile,
your facial hair closely cropped.

I would hug you so hard.

We are all here at this conference
trying to find a way
to regain some meaning in our lives
without our kids
physically by our sides.

They say
you are closer to us
than we think.

Well,
I am listening

and looking around,
waiting for you
to walk through the door.

A New Relationship

A new relationship.
That's what my therapist told me.
I can cultivate a new relationship with my son.
That sounds…
crazy.

A new relationship?

I'd rather have the old one back,
thank you.
But that is not possible.
It will never be.
The new reality is what I am faced with.
The new relationship.

How does that work?
Can I really still continue
my relationship with him?

PART 2

THE SHIFT

Meditation Table

A friend made
a small table for me.
It's only 16 inches tall.
I used one of your awesome

button-down shirts
(the soft blue one with the
small pearly white designs on it)
as a tablecloth,

and on it I have placed
two candles,
two rose quartz crystals,
as well as

jasper and selenite,
a small crucifix with Jesus on it,
a mini Buddha figurine,
and an angel.

Not to mention the shot glass
Nick had made for us
with the cartoon drawing of you
that your good buddy created.
(Ha-ha!)

I sit in front of it
on a small cushion.

It's simple.
Just a start.

Just a place to find myself,
and God.
And you.
A rendezvous.

I feel grateful.

Be Still

All that matters is this moment.
I strive to know more and more
and more.
I am impatient.
And yet

all there is to know
is already within my soul.
I will discover it—
day by day.

Eric is not gone.
He is here
in my heart
in my soul
in my memories
in my eyes and ears
and sometimes
in my dreams.

I am learning to connect.
I am learning to just
be still
breathe
listen.

Don't try to do anything.
That's hard for me—

I am always trying to do something

but I trust
what I am learning.

This moment
is all.

In My Mind's Eye

Again
I am here
I am right here

I see your dark eyes
They watch me
Your eyes smile
You are pensive
I remember that contemplative look

But you are not right here
Right in front of me
I reach out
But my hand does not exist
In the same world
As your face
Your eyes
There is a space

How do I cross that space?
How do I connect my hand with your face?

I long to touch you
I long to run my fingers across
The facial hair along your jawline
Or down the bridge of your nose
Or across your dark eyebrows
I long to tug on your earlobe

Just the gentlest little tug
Just like I used to do
When I drove you in the car
When you were younger
You would look at me and ask me
Why I did that
I would say,
"That means I love you."

That space
I wish to cross that space
Between the land of time
And the world of no time
That beautiful place
That place of bliss
That place where we were together
Even before we came here
Home
That home
The one where you are right now
And where I will meet you again
Some day
One day
When it is time

Until then, I watch you
In my mind's eye
I see you
You look at me
I smile at you and you smile at me

You are quiet
I am still
We are apart...

Yet we are connected
By that silver thread
My heart to yours
It is inseverable
We remain linked
Locked
Together
Forever

I am here

I see you

I see you

In my mind's eye.

Numbers

I am noticing
These numbers
That feel like a connection to you

They just show up
When I'm driving along
Talking to you in the car
Listening to your music

A license plate
A billboard
The address on a sign
For a yard sale
The final sale on the gasoline pump

No coincidences
They say

What—
Is that a smile on my face?

Mentor

In the dream
I was watching you.
You were alive.
I knew you were going to die
but you didn't seem to know
or maybe it wasn't a concern to you.
You were hanging out with your friends.

You looked at me
and noticed I was pensive.
You asked, "What?"
I said, "Nothing."

Then suddenly
I was in a room
where someone else was playing your drums.
You were next to him
watching him
and at one point
when the drummer wasn't
getting the rhythm right
you gently took the sticks from him
and showed him how to do it
then gave the sticks back to him
and let him continue.

I do believe you are guiding us.

Clouds

How do you do it?
Make those clouds into the shape of an E?
I saw three already today
and I've seen others in the past weeks.
I even saw your initials—
EC—
right next to each other.

How do you do it?

Another time when I was driving
I was nudged to look up
and there in the sky
was the outline of a heart—
maybe shaped by an airplane—
but perfect
and beautiful
and it made me smile.
Did you put it in my head to look up?

And on two other occasions,
while dreamily watching
those incredible clouds float by,
they seemed to take the shape of your face.
Your face.
In the sky.
Looking down at me.
I assumed I was imagining it.

But now
I'm beginning to wonder.

Transformation

I am not the same as I was before.
And I never will be.

But nothing remains the same.
Everything changes.

Those adorable little children
I had in the '90s
have all changed.
They have big bodies now,
or
(in Eric's case)
a spiritual one.

As our bodies age
they don't look the same as they used to.
But we are each still the same person.

Eric's spirit body is not the same
as the one he used here.
But he is still the same person.
He is still Eric.

Zildjian

That Zildjian sticker
I saw on the car in front of me
as I drove home last night...
was that from you?

I had never seen one of those stickers before.
I had just been asking you what to get you
for Christmas
(I still talk to you every day)
which I could then donate after the holidays.

So I went to Guitar Center
to look at the cymbals
just like we used to.
I asked you which one I should get
keeping the budget in mind all the while
just like we used to.

I picked one out
a Zildjian crash
and took it to the register
and paid for it
feeling my heavy heart
feeling you with me.

As I left the store
and walked across the parking lot
there

right there
was your car
an old black Ford Explorer Sport.
I don't see many of those anymore.

I stopped
and stared for a moment
feeling a little shocked
and more than a bit elated
and as I looked closer
I saw
up in the left corner
of the windshield
another sticker.

It said DW.
That was the brand of drum kit
you had just bought
a few months before you left us.
This car belonged to a drummer
just like you.

I stood there for a bit longer
who knows how long
and drank up that feeling
that you
were right there

with me
purchasing a Zildjian cymbal

as we had always done.

Let Me Get This Straight

So, let me get this straight…

I am here
and you are there,
but you are here
with me
always,
and I search to understand
as much as I can
with my little human brain
to know God,
to know myself,
my purpose here,
and to understand why you're not here
physically.

But you *are* here
spiritually
and I learn
to expand my awareness,
to look beyond my five senses,
to develop my intuition
so I can be closer to you,
to God,
to myself.

And so I meditate
and I read
and I listen
to the teachers of expanded consciousness.

Yet,
as much time as I spend looking out there
and in here
for you,
I am also supposed to be here on Earth
in my body,
to fulfill
my purpose,
to live,
to enjoy,
as you told me.

It's kind of a balancing act—
these two worlds.
I continue to search,
to understand.
I can do it
as long as you are with me,
surrounding me

and I know you are.

Always.

Birds

The hummingbird
that stopped me
on my way down the schoolyard steps
hovered right in front of my face
for a long time.

The finches outside the bathroom window
perched on the wire just a few feet away.
They are there every morning for me.
I know each one of them.
I know their songs.
They bring me joy.
They were never there before.

Those two crows
that I said hello to from the porch
as they sat on the cable wire above the driveway—
they flew into the neighboring tree.

Then…
as I backed out of the driveway,
they came back to the porch
and soared right toward me,
together,
barely skimming the car,
swooping up over the windshield
and away.
I gasped

and felt goosebumps of joy.
Was that you?
And who were you with?

How did you do it?
I know it has something to do with you.
I feel such peace,
such connection with you.

I don't know how it works,
but I'll take it.

216 days

You did it again
you crossed the veil
between Earth and the spirit world
for just a moment

I heard you

lying in my bed at night
crying as I always do
missing you so much

I did the self-guided meditation
that I often do
a way for me to meet with you
even if it is my imagination
it doesn't matter
it always makes me feel better

but this time
this time…
As I imagined being at our meeting place
at a seaside village
overlooking the sparkling blue-green water
that rolls over the white sand

I looked in the distance
And saw you coming toward me
I longed to run toward you

So I could hug you

Just then
I heard something
in my ear
not from the imaginary meeting place
but right in my physical ear
while I lay in bed

you said
I'm right here mom

I was not startled
I just knew
it was you

I was overcome with a peace
a calmness
a safety
an assuredness
that I had never felt before

and immediately drifted off to sleep.

Still With Me

The other night
you came to me in a dream.
You walked beside me
through a park
and reached over to hold my hand,
assuring me that you were still here,
still with me.

When you left your physical body
I was so scared.
I thought, "Maybe that is it—
I will never know you again."

I'm so glad I was wrong.

I feel you all around
in the breezes that caress me.
I see you in the clouds
and in the rising sun.
And I hear you in the music,
in every drumbeat.

Thank you, my son, for all the love
you have given us
and continue to give us.
Love is never-ending.
We are still connected—
heart to heart,

soul to soul—
by our Love.

Hello

I reach over to turn the knob that turns on the air conditioner in my classroom.

And one second before I get there, the air conditioner goes on! This happens over and over again as the days pass. Sometimes I'm not even near the knob and the AC just goes on. None of my students are aware of this strange phenomenon. I ask the teacher who was in the room last year if this ever happened to her when she was in that room. She says no and that it sounds a little spooky! I ask my brother who has a good amount of knowledge of heating and air conditioning systems if there could be some explanation—the AC system is old, after all. He could not think of why that would happen. So, I have left it to my original gut feeling that you are just letting me know again that you are around. Just a little hello as I go about my day.

So, hello. You're hilarious.

You Were There

Your sister was a bridesmaid
In the wedding of
One of her good friends.
It was the first your dad and I had attended
Since you left this Earth.

Ah, the sweetness of a wedding.
The blue sky
The soft green grass
The pink satin dresses
The black tuxedos with crisp white shirts
The chiseled young faces
Of the bridal party
The joy and the charm.
Your sister looked absolutely beautiful.

I tried not to think about how
You would never get to experience this.

Tried not to think about it.
Tried not to think about it.

But when the groom walked down the aisle
With his mother at his side
I could not hold it back any longer.

As quietly as I could
I stood there with fat tears filling my eyes

And streaming down my face
Knowing I could get away with it
Because, after all, we were at a wedding.

Yet,
In some strange way
As I viewed the scene with my eyes
I could also see you
In my mind's eye
Quite clearly.

You,
In your dark suit and blue shirt and black tie
Looking right at me
Smiling, sweet, and handsome
Letting me know
You were right there with me.

You stayed for 15 minutes or so.
Then the image of you faded
As we all continued on with this celebration
Of the bride and groom.

But I still felt you with me
Felt your love
And the comfort you gave me.
Your presence
Was undeniable.

Floating

I used to walk with my feet firmly on the ground.
Then you left your body
And headed for home in the Heavens.
When you did, I floated upwards
And began to sail the skies
In search of You
In search of Meaning
In search of God
In search of Truth.

All is changed.
All is bittersweet.

I look down upon the Earth as I float
And see a new perspective.
I feel calm
I feel peace
I feel reconnected
To stillness
To Peace.

Every day I touch down upon the Earth
And do what I am here to do
With You
With Meaning
With God
With Truth
With You.

A new perspective.

And at night, I'm free to float
To touch the stars
Untethered to life's burdens.
I float
I sing
I fly
With you.

Spiritual Hug

In my dream last night
I stood there
Serene
Alone

I closed my eyes
And asked for your hug
And your energy and spirit were there
In a less than solid form
But still discernable
Still there
And you hugged me
Warmly

Last night
In your room
You asked
What do you believe?

That one I will answer
Over time…

You Lived Life

Driving home today
listening to the music you loved
and played on your radio show…
all the drummers sound like you.

Thinking about
all the music festivals, concerts, gigs
you attended constantly.
I remember how it sort of bothered me
that you just had to go to yet another
music performance.
I'd argue with you (only a bit)
but you still went.

I am so glad you did.

Now,
more than ever
I get how important that all was to you.
It *was* you
and I appreciate that you went out
and lived life.
You enjoyed as much as you could.

Clearly you did.

I didn't want you to go to
eight more countries

after you finished your
study abroad in Madrid.
Another four weeks!
I just wanted you to come home.
But you stayed.

I am so glad you did.

You tell me you are around.
You tell me to live my life—

Yes
I will
I will
For you
For me.

Because that is what you would do.

Oddly
I know you even better now
since you transitioned into spirit.

Madrid

One Year

One whole fucking year.
Sorry.
I still have to say it like that.

I get where you are.
I get this may be the plan.
I believe you were meant to be here.
After all,
you were a surprise to us all.

I have no doubt you made the world a better place,
that you changed us all
for the better.
I am grateful,
I am,
so grateful
that we had you here for almost 24 ½ years.

If I had been told
before you were born
that I could l have the most handsome, loving son,
a son that would charm us all
with his talents and humor
and would treat us all with the utmost respect
and surround us with love
but that I could only have you
for 24 years, 5 months, and 19 days,
I would still want you

because I would never want
to have never known you.

We are all blessed
because you were here,
because you loved us.
You live on
in all of our memories,
our photos and videos,
in your music,
and in each and every one of us.

Your memory will not die
because we will continue to speak your name
every day.
Every day.
We will talk about all the incredible times
we spent with you
and I know—
I *know*—
you are still here with us.
I feel you with me.
I see you in my mind's eye
constantly
and sometimes you visit us in our dreams.

And I thank you for that
for being with us
for hanging around
for watching over us

for continuing to love us.
You blessed us when you were here physically
and you still bless us in spirit.

And I know—
I know—
I will be with you again someday
we all will
but in the meantime we will honor you
by doing the work we were put here to do
and by continuing to spread
the love you gave us.

The Music, The Dance

When I am missing you
I find you
in the music.
You always said I could find you there.

I hear the drumbeat.
That is you.
That is where I find you.
In the music.

I thought I knew music,
but you taught me more about it.
The connection was made.
We shared the love of music
in our souls.
Our souls knew music.

I didn't realize how much we both connected to music
until I saw our old texts.
You'd send me something to listen to
and I'd send you a song back.

The music.

I miss you
so I find the music you appreciated,
you enjoyed,
you resonated with,

and I play that music
and my soul resonates with it, too.
I close my eyes and I move
to the music,
to the instrument,
to the drumbeat.
The dance in me comes out,
integrated with the music.
The dance I learned so long ago—
I feel it come alive—
as I hear the music.
Your music.

I feel something as I move.
I feel me.
I feel life.
I feel truth.
I feel that all that matters is this moment.
This moment,
the music,
you,
me,
the dance.
My arms reach and curve.
They float and pull.
My legs support me,
step around and turn me.
I am strong.

And then the music slows.

I see you.
We come together
and dance
a slow dance,
Mother and Son,
the one I planned to dance one day
with you at your wedding.
Slowly stepping,
slowly circling.
It is eternal.
The love between us is there.
Is forever.

I know you are with me.
You tell me, *I'm here, Mom.*
I have heard you.

Time stands still.
I am fine.
I am peaceful.
I am with you.
And you are with me.

When I am missing you
I know where to find you.
You are not far.
You are right here.
In the music.

PART 3

THE AWAKENING

Expansion

When you left your physical body
I expanded.

I had to.

Because in that expansion
is where I find you.

Gestation

Book
after book
after book
after book

Grasping at something
anything
a thread
a breath
of hope
of truth

of you

Swirling colors of
my Self
my spirit
my soul
reformulating
reverberating
realizing
shifting
changing
rediscovering
who I really am.

A hidden truth
bursting forth

an enlightening
an aligning
a resonance
of what is real
what is true
what is love.

Book
after book
after book
after book

I am emerging.

New Journal

Let's begin this new journal
me and you.
Have you seen me
trying to connect?
I'm trying not to try so hard
Ha!
But I love, enjoy
talking to you
and thinking about you.

I'm ready now,
ready to connect this way with you every day.
It is comforting
because I know you are here.

Your sister is here right now with me
in the living room—
me in the maroon armchair,
she on the couch with her laptop.
But I know you already know.
You see us.

I like to imagine where you are in the room…
on the other armchair?
On the other floral-print couch, the smaller one?
On the floor with your dogs?
Do you stare at us?
Smile at us?
I bet you do.

Shifting

My whole belief system
Is changing
Shifting
Flowing
How can it not?

Not only as a result
Of all the books I have read
To help me cope
Books about death
And life after death
About near death experiences
And spirituality

But also with the
Dreams we have all been receiving
And signs from birds
And clouds
And visions
Of you next to me at the party
Whispering in my ear

There's more
There's something more

As I sit in silence
In meditation
Listening to my heart

Listening to
God
It feels truthful
It feels right

I am shifting
I am evolving
This journey has been horribly painful
Unbearably devastating
Brutal

And…
Amazingly beautiful.

I Want to Understand

I prayed,
I want to understand how to serve
using my gifts
my love
my pain.
And this came to me:

Trust
all is as it should be.
You have seen those
leave this world early,
or so it may seem.
Many of them are not known
throughout the world,
but you see them
creating such a large impact
because of all the small
(or not so small)
beautiful things they have done.
They just *are.*
The same can be said for you.

You don't have to figure it out.
Just be.

Just
be
you.

You are enough.

Hunter Gatherer

I am a hunter
Searching for that which
My heart cries out for
Some sustenance
For my weakened soul
Beaten down by grief and despair
Confused and befuddled
With no idea of
Which way I am to go
For the path, once clear
Is in utter destruction.

I am a gatherer
Of books, of words, of philosophies
Of spiritual food
To help put back together
That which has been shattered
To rebuild the God-forsaken annihilation
Of what I thought life was
I gather as much and
As quickly as I can
For I am starving
Just trying to survive.

I am a thresher
Separating the wheat from the chaff
Sifting through all
I have brought into my suffering heart and soul

Maintaining what is useful to me
What is healing
A balm
Tossing out that which does not resonate
And keeping that which does
As I am slowly nourished
By the new understandings
That ring true for me
I begin to find the strength to
Stand up straight again
To walk, to look around
To nod my head
To smile
A newfound hint of purpose
Something within
Begins to illuminate
Possibly even sing
Ever so softly, sweetly
A peace that remains
Amidst the continuing absurdities
All around.

I am a planter
I take what has been given me
By the teachers in the books,
The words, the philosophies
The spiritual food
And share it
Sow it
Whenever I can

Wherever I can
The gift is meant to be given
My journey is your journey
My healing is your healing.

When You Left This Earth

When you left this Earth
I was so scared
I thought maybe that was it
That I would never know you again

I am so glad I was wrong

I still feel you all around
In the cool breezes
And the dampness of the rain
I see you in the clouds
And in the rising sun
I hear you in the
Crash of the ocean's waves
And in the music—
In every drumbeat

Thank you
My son
For all you have given me
And continue to give me…

Let It Flow

In the silence
I heard you say…

Let it flow
We write together
The words
Are breathed into you
They are the exhale
Of the heavens
A gift to share
Your pen soothes
All those
Who read your words.

Dare I Say...

In the immediate aftermath
Of my son's departure
I found
Somewhere in the midst of
My deep pain
A stillness
An unexpected peace

Everything stopped
Nothing mattered anymore

And in this abrupt hold
This megalithic boulder
That rolled directly into life's path
I had…
Dare I say…

The opportunity
The blessing
Of seeing everything around me
In a new light

A pure light

The light of rebirth

The light of something great

The light of God.

Timelessness

Slowing down allows me
To savor the moment
Then time can stand still

And in the timelessness
There is no past
No future
All is here now
In this moment

And you are here.

Ripple Effect

You came to this Earth
and touched us all
as a son
brother
grandson
cousin
nephew
and friend.
Our lives would never be the same
because we now knew you.

You left this Earth
and your leaving
touched us all
even more.
We did not know our time
together with you here
would be so short.
Our lives will never be the same
because we once knew you.

But you are here with us still
in the music you left behind
in our hearts
and our memories
and in all the photographs and videos.

You cannot be erased.

You had a huge impact here on us all.

Your impact still reverberates
and will continue
forever.

Memories

Memories
cannot be erased.
They are all there.
All still right there.
They are part of our soul,
our being—
certainly, our human persona.
We need them here.
They help us on this Earthly journey.

We can keep the good ones.
When times are tough
we can remember
the joys.
We hold them dear;
we tattoo them onto our hearts.
They help us cope;
they help us navigate our way
through this life.

And the bad memories
we can choose to let go of.
We can set them sail
on a toy boat.
They float down a river,
adrift,
away.
When we get to the Other Side,

we won't need them anymore.
We will have all we need,
for we will be with all our loved ones
in perpetual bliss.

A Few Lessons Learned So Far

I can put forth the intention to heal,
take an active role in healing.
It is up to me.

Why me?
Why *not* me?
I am not the first mother to experience
this kind of loss
and I won't be the last.
"Why" gets you nowhere.

Instead, ask how…
How will I survive this?
How can I have a spiritual relationship
with my child now
instead of a physical one?

I have learned that
just *being* here is enough.
I don't need to be *doing*.

Know who you are.
Everyone's truth is their own truth.
Turn inward to the essence
of your own soul.

When in deep grief,
just go outside.

Look at something beautiful in nature—
Breathe,

look at the sky,
the clouds,
the trees,
the flowers,
the birds.
Be in the moment.

Paradox

One year and seven months
after Eric's transition,
my mom went home
to Heaven
to be with my brother,
her son,
as well as her grandson,
my son,
and many others
who had gone before her.
Grief
again
came to visit.

Three weeks later,
a baby was born.
He was my soon-to-be
son-in-law's new nephew.
My own son, Nick,
the godfather,
was there
to cut the umbilical cord.

The joy,
the miracle,
of a newborn baby
is palpable,
is the stuff that dreams are made of.

That same day,
we got the news
that my sister-in-law
had stage 3 breast cancer
and the cancer was spreading rapidly.
Shock and sadness
filled our hearts
and such loving support
flooded our text thread.

Such a paradox,
the beauty
in both
the pain of death
and the miracle of birth.

Love is the glue
that connects
those seemingly contradictory experiences.
Love is all.

When All Was Sweet

Sometimes the memories
Hold me together like glue

Sometimes
When the world swirls around me
In uncontrollable chaos
And confusion
I can look at a photo
And go back to a time
When all was sweet
And well

I can hold it
And I can grasp it
And it is mine

No one can take
The sweet memories
Away.

Unexpected Grace

Eric
when you moved to Heaven,
died,
I was angry at God.
Why wouldn't I be?
After all,
He took you away from me.
Right?

I had learned
years ago
that God was an old man in the sky
who sat in judgement
and answered your prayers
if
and only if
you deserved it.
Otherwise,
He ignored you.

And I thought I was a good person.
I thought I was doing
what I was supposed to be doing.
So then why
did God
do this to me?

That was the God I knew,

and somehow this notion
no longer made sense to me.
I had to let it go.

So I have been reading books
written by so many people
of varied faiths
and experiences
and philosophies
and I have pondered each one
and pulled out
that which resonates as truth
for me.

And little by little,
like a sprouting seed
that begins to feel the sun upon its face,
I let God out of the tiny box
I was taught She lived in
and allowed God to emerge in fullness.

God is the Creator,
the Divine Source of all Love.
God does not deem us worthy or unworthy,
listen to some prayers
and ignore others.
If this is so
then where is the love?

I wouldn't even do that to my own child.
We are always worthy.

God does not take from us.
God has given us all we need.
She is in all of creation
and in each other
and in ourselves.
God is the power of Love
God is in every act of kindness
exploding with compassion

I saw that
in the weeks after my son left this world
in all the caring people
that surrounded us.
God was there.
Right there
in the space between everything.
I understand this now.
I feel this
in my heart
and words cannot fully express
what I now know.

It is beautiful.
Somehow,
in a way I don't understand
beauty has come
from the worst possible thing I could imagine.

Cosmos

In my dream
I stood in a non-descript place
Hands to my side
Chin up a little

I telepathically asked you
For a hug
I felt you
Put your arms around me
And hug me

You had a form
But it was ethereal
It felt like we were in
The cosmos

I wanted to stay there.

I Am Still Here

I did not ask for this
The human part of me
Never
Ever
In a million years
Wanted to experience a child of mine
Transition before I did

I have heard some say
That our souls did choose this
Maybe so
There was a quiet resonance in my heart
When I heard this
And over time I came to believe
It to be true
Though not everyone does

Regardless
If this is what has happened
If this is what has been given to me
Or what I have chosen
Then let me take it and run with it
Let me take all of it
And have it turn me into
The very, very best self
I can be

If somehow

I am to live this life
As a mother with one child
On the Other Side

Then rather than let it break me
Let it build me and expand me
Let it take the broken parts of me
And allow the light inside of me
My truest self
To shine through
Bright and bold
Let it teach me
All that I came here to learn
Let it teach me
That there is more than this
Let it turn me into a warrior
Of love
Of hope
Of service
And of compassion

To honor my son
I will do this
To honor my mother and grandmother before me
Whose children also passed before them
I will do this

I will do this with my son on my left
My angels on my right
My ancestors behind me

Mother Earth below me
And God above me

Show me
Teach me
Guide me
I prevail.

Connections

I am learning a lot
with this new life that I never asked for.

We have a physical and spiritual connection
with those we love when they are alive on Earth.
We maintain the spiritual connection
when they transition.

The river of grief will take us to healing,
which means it will take us to
a new connection with them.
We loved them in their physical presence;
now we continue to love them in their physical absence.

They still love us
and we still love them.

In life, we could look over and say
"I love you."
In death, we can still do that.

Just tell them.
They hear you.

I love you, Eric.
I love you, Eric.
I love you Eric.

That bond will never break.

Snow Globe

If the moment is joyful
feel the joy,
and if the moment is sorrowful
feel the sorrow.
There is beauty in each
and there is God in each.
We gather in joy to dance and celebrate
and we gather in sorrow to mourn.

Some hold back in their expression of joy
for fear of falling too hard
when the inevitable pain comes to visit,
numbing out the pain,
denying it,
or pushing it away.
Protection from life itself.

Life contains both—
a balance,
a snow globe of experiences.

A wise one once said,
Do not be afraid
for I am with you.
Always
in each moment.
Live each moment.

Panorama

What do you do
when your hopes are dashed,
when they've been slammed to the ground,
and broken into more pieces
than you can count?

What do you do?

Do you stare at them for days and weeks
and mourn their demise?
Do you step around them and see them
from another perspective?
Do you stamp on them in a rage?
Be careful as you will likely cut your feet.

Do you kick them aside,
clearing a new path for yourself?
Do you turn your back on them
and swear to have nothing more to do with them again?

Do you speak to them?
Do you say, *You disappointed me?*
Or do you say, *Thank you?*
Do you sweep them up and throw them away
or send them down the river?

Or maybe…
maybe…

you take all the pieces
and pile them up
and stand on them
as they now provide leverage
for you to look out,
look around,
and see new possibilities,
endless possibilities,
that you would not have otherwise seen.

More, Not Less

Who am I now
without my child physically present?

I have heard so many other parents
ask this same question
after the transition of their child.

I did live my life before he came to us.
I was someone before I had children.

Then I became enriched
with the birth of each one of my children.

And now
without Eric,
who am I?

Five years ago, I would've said,
"Nobody."

But now,
strangely,
I can say that I am actually
even more,
not less.

With each new experience,
good or bad,
I become more.
Not less.

The Love Remains

I am no longer in that deep dark abyss
Somehow
It was actually possible
To climb out
Just enough
To see
To know
That the light is still there.

Healing is possible.

I still grieve
I always will.

But I can grieve peacefully
With more love than pain.

Words and thoughts are powerful
It's up to me
I can say I will never heal
Or I can say
That maybe
Maybe
I will
I can open the door.

When our time here is done
We go home

But the relationship with those still here on Earth
Continues
Because the love continues
The love remains.

A Thousand Days

I have survived the worst
And still
I am grateful
I have all I need
It is enough
It is plenty

Sometimes
I worry
That something so painful
So heart-wrenching
Can happen again

No point in worrying

I shift my focus
To silvery hues of gratitude
To that which I do have
Instead of that which I don't

And I take all that I've experienced
All the jagged pain
The rocky hardships
The barbed challenges
And spin them into gold.

PART 4

THE HEALING

All Good Gifts

The birds
Beautiful
Free

They are a gift to us
As we work through our challenges

They are a respite when we are weary

The trees
The flowers
The mountains
The sky
The clouds
All gifts
To help us
As we navigate our way
Through life

All teachers
Of how to be

To just
Be

Healing Tree

That tree
That magnificent pine tree
In front of the house
The one I was drawn to lie under
Right after Eric transitioned.

I think possibly
She had called me
Beckoned me
To come outside
So that I could lie under her
and heal.

At the time
I was too filled with fresh grief
To even notice
How I ended up out there
Flat on my back
Gazing up through her awesome branches
Into the pure blue sky
Finding some semblance
Of peace.

But now
Thinking back to
Those unbearably painful first months

I think
I believe
That tree's spirit
Called me
And gave me her medicine.

Those Birds

Walking through the parking lot after my therapy appointment, this hummingbird flew right in front of me, stopping me in my tracks. He stared at me for about 10 seconds, then flew up a few feet and back down again from one side to the other, swooping back and forth 3 times before flying away. I felt joy. Those birds make me chuckle—finches hanging outside my bathroom window, crows flying alongside my car, mockingbirds chirping so loudly that your grandmother and I once had to stop our conversation and look until they finished what they had to say. Yes, son, you got my attention. Yes, I think of you right away. I love those birds. They bring me to the moment, this moment, which I have learned is all that matters.

Moonrise

I saw the moon rise tonight
Right outside my bedroom window
I spied her behind a distant tree
Her yellow-orange glow caught my eye
We gazed at each other
And I thanked her for her love

As she
Oh so slowly
Crept upward into the sky
It occurred to me
That if everyone
Every person
Could just stop for a moment
Turn off their TVs
Put down their phones
Stop finding a reason to argue and fight
Come outside
And just look up at the moon
Without speaking
Without worrying about the cares of the world

Then
The world would begin to heal
The vibration of love
That each person would feel
In that moment
Would send a ripple around the world

An energy
That would be felt by all
And for that moment
There would be peace on Earth

So powerful you are, Moon
Thank you for your healing
Thank you for your love.

The Clouds Teach Me

The clouds teach me
Their form is constantly changing
I can look at their beauty in this moment
And one minute later
The form will have changed a little

Everything changes
Nothing remains the same
It is still that cluster of water molecules
That sometimes takes the shape of a cloud
Other times rain and water
Other times ice and snow

Yes
It is the same cluster of particles

I don't need to grieve
When the clouds look different today
Than they did yesterday

They are still the same clouds
In a different form
And if I don't see any clouds
This day
Or the next
I know I will still see them
Again one day.

Wedding Thoughts

All day I took in each moment
Stopping and looking around

I breathed in the jasmine
That was around the archway
That led us into the girls' dressing rooms
Bath houses as they called them

I watched a multitude
Of monarch butterflies flit by
Dancing
And loving their existence

I gazed up at the sky—
A crystal clear blue
With scattered wispy clouds
Playfully floating and watching us

I felt the cool breeze wrap its arms around us
Throughout the ceremony

I felt loved
It was all love
All love
And you were there
I know this was a gift.

There They Are Again

There they are again
those birds
zipping through the sky
darting this way and that.
It must be playtime.
Their joy is palpable.
I can feel it.
I cannot see their faces
but I do believe
if I could
I would see
that they are laughing.

Mountain Meditation

I gaze at you
And you gaze at me
I absorb myself into your contours
Your crevices
The supple folds of your hillside
Like drapery.

Teach me.

What advice do you have for me?
You are strong
Solid
Steadfast
Unwavering in your expression
Of who you are
You don't worry about pleasing anyone
Or doing anything
Or getting things done
Or doing what you should.

You just *are*
And that is enough.

No need to look like a different mountain
No need to compare yourself to another
All that you are
Is enough.
Thank you for guiding me

Thank you for affirming me
Thank you for gazing back at me
With such love.

I hope that I may carry you with me
Wherever I go
That I may hold you in my heart
And know you are always with me
Even when you are covered by clouds.

Waters

I sit
in front
of a waterfall.

As I take in the love
I realize
the connection
to the waters of the world
to the waters of the oceans
the rivers
the seas and lakes.

And as I know
for a fact
that the molecules of water
never leave our atmosphere
I realize that each droplet has been here
since the beginning of time.

I realize these are the same waters
that every person
throughout history
has been a part of…
from Jesus and his Mother Mary
to my ancestors
and my son…
they all have touched
these same waters

whether in the Black Sea
the Sea of Galilee
the Pacific Ocean
or the snows of Andorra.

Even the clouds in the sky
carry these same water molecules
from eons of time.

And as I gaze up at these
white powder puffs of $H2O$
I am overcome with awe
and the grandeur of it all
how elegant
how loving
how comforting.

We are connected by the waters
of Mother Earth
of Creation
of All That Is.

Drummer in the Sky

I saw you in the sky this morning
Through my bedroom window
In the clouds.

A side view
Of a sitting figure
One arm reaching out
Holding a drumstick
Hitting a drum
Above it—a cymbal
The large one called a "ride"
I knew it was that one
We used to go together
to buy cymbals for your birthday.

I stared for a long time
The other clouds shifted a bit
Around you
But you stayed the same
The sun was just coming up
Right below
The golden glow rose up and lit you
Along with the drum and cymbal
In a beautiful heavenly light.

I was tempted to grab my phone
To snap a picture
But I was mesmerized

Motionless
And I didn't want to miss a thing.

Just then
Six birds flew across the sky
Right in front of you
Six
One for each of us
No coincidence.

I sat still
In the silence
I felt peace
Knowing I was meant to see that
It was your "hello"
And your way of letting me know
You still play drums
In paradise
I got to taste that for a moment
I got a glimpse.

My heart is full to the brim
With joy.

Delicate Dance

The delicate dance
Of the leaves
In the gentle breeze
Ground me
Fill me
Remind me
That grace and love
Are always here
They can be found
In each subtle movement

And in that perfect moment
Is peace

Just look
Take it in
Take the time
To be still
To breathe in
And breathe out
To experience
To just...
Be

Simple Joys

It's the simple things
That fill my soul…

Water the flowers
Kiss the rose
Gaze at the sky
Play the drum.

Feel the wind
Touch the earth
Taste the sweetness
Of the invisible arms of love.

Therein lies the joy.

This Day

The clouds—
White, soft, elegant,
Against the endless blue sky—
Watched over us
Knowing this day
Had been long anticipated.

And from these heavens
Flowed grace,
Flowed love,
A magic that
Touched each of us
With an immeasurable joy.
So silent was this flow,
So unsuspecting,
Yet somewhere deep inside
We knew
This was a day like no other.

The jasmine knew.
They celebrated with exhalations
Of their delicate scent
Surrounding, enveloping
Every one of us
As we inhaled their joy.

The monarch butterflies knew.
They flitted and danced

With unbounded delight
Soaring in all directions,
Catching our eyes.
One could almost see their smiles.

The goldfinches knew.
Delicately perched on twigs and branches,
Joyously proclaiming their delight
With sweet songs and calls
And effortless flights from tree to tree.

Each moment held the enchantment
Of a thousand days.
Each smile spoke affection
And unmitigated bliss.
Each exhalation of breath
Connected one to another.

And both of you…
Your eyes spoke
Without words
Of a love so deep
Of a passion that surpasses time
Of a devotion and rejoicing
Greater than any words could ever convey,
Two hearts beating as one.
Just you two
Radiating peace and love
With the brilliance of diamonds
Received by all those whose eyes rested upon

Your joy.
And we all walked
Floated
Inches above the ground
Throughout this enchanted day

Time stood still
As we took in
These moments
Of grace
Of gratitude
Of blessing.

And at night's end
A million stars above
Kissed us goodnight
As the memory of this magical day
Soared into eternity.

Hidden in Plain Sight

Your instinct compels you
To turn toward beauty
Truth
A wave of luxurious bliss
Is what you look for

It is here
Right beside you
Look around
It is in this moment
Hidden in plain sight

The sun beckons you to know
What is in your heart
You are bathed in this light
Of the rising sun
Let it wash over you

Six birds gracefully fly by
Against the enflamed colors
Of the sunrise
A backdrop of promise

Let this moment always remind you
Always stay with you
That all is Divine
All is Love.

The Roses are Magnificent

The roses are magnificent
They fill my senses
They are intricate
And soft
The colors hold me
At full attention
My eyes
Draw in all they offer.

Their scent
Subtly intoxicating
Charms me
Disarms me
I surrender to the bouquet.

I draw close to one sweet blossom
And let it kiss my cheek
Have you ever let a rose kiss your cheek?
It will change you
Transform you
In the best way ever.

Contained Within

Inside a tree
Are circles
Proof of all the years
The tree has existed
A new circle for each year
A circle of life
All that the tree has lived
Is still there
In its circles.

As with each one of us—
We grow
And all that we have lived
Remains contained within
The sweetness
The pain
The love
The relationships
None of them are gone
They are all still a part of us.

Cloud Angel

Clarity
flows though me.
At times I feel its kiss.
It is sweet.

The clouds covered the sky this morning.
If I were an artist
they would have been the result
of thick paint
moved around with my fingertips
swirls of white and gray
creating various shades
with a few spots of blue sky passing through.

I stood outside on the back deck
mesmerized,
the cool morning air
caressing my face,
tilted up to the heavens,
when suddenly
within the clouds
the form of an angel became clear.
Not just an outline—
she was there, present,
angled slightly to her right,
arms outstretched,
her right hand appearing
to reach softly for something,

her hair flowing behind her to the left,
and the subtle shape of wings
around her.

There she was,
my angel,
offering me the gift
of a glimpse of her
which I had been requesting.
Oh, so sweet,
the clarity of that moment
before the clouds moved on
and slowly swept her away.

Present

The present is a present
the gift of this moment
the loveliness of this moment
the presence of The Most Holy.

And in the exact moment
that I look up from writing this
I see three different flocks of parrots
migrate across the sky in front of me
about a mile or more away
flying from left to right
south to north
their bodies just specks in the sky
yet the movement of their wings
still detectable.

They have no idea
what joy they bring me
just being who they are.

I feel the connection.

Cloudship

I sail the skies
In a cloudship
Soft and white
Unburdened
Untethered
And free.

And as I do
I find the truth
Of who I am…
I am joy.

You sail with me
We have never been apart
Our course is undetermined
Adventure flows in every moment.

Our smiles are never-ending
Our ocean is the sky
Our cloudship is navigated
Effortlessly…
Peace.

PART 5

THE RISE

Look Around

These last few years
I have come across some deeply inspiring teachers
Who have taught me profound truths
About living this life

Here's one:

Every day
I stop several times
For a few moments
To just be
To breathe
To look around

This is our inner purpose
To enjoy
To love
Each moment

I guess Eric already knew that
Deep down
He used to do that
And so he left that for us
For all of us

I appreciate that, my son
Every day my intention
Is to look around
And be amazed

Who I Am

Who am I?
Who are You, God?
Why are we here?
What's the point?
Why isn't Eric still here?

I have asked these questions
since May 12, 2017.
I believe I have received
some answers
on this new journey
of awareness.
But there are a million more
where those came from.

I still strive
to know
the Truth.

Each day
I peel away
a little more
of anything that keeps me
from knowing
who I really am.

I am.
I am.
I surrender my ego.

Discovering
who
I am.

The Egg

Do not be afraid to be broken
for that's when the miracle can be realized.

The egg,
the yolk within the egg,
holds so much potential
and the chick grows within.

But unless the shell is broken
and the chick breaks out
it will never realize that potentiality.

It will never be
who it was meant to be.

Growing Pains

Here we are
On this Earth
Visiting

Our real home
Is Heaven
Where we came from

But while we're here
We are to grow
To learn
To love
To create
To remember
To know the truth

The joys are great
But it is so hard here
At least we grow from the pain

And all the while
We need to trust
Trust
That's what it means
To have
Faith.

Bridge

I breathe

I place my hand over my heart
For it is a bridge
A connector

I now stand on that bridge
With my arms outstretched
Holding the hands
Of my loved ones here on Earth
With one hand
And the hands of those in spirit
With my other hand

I am connected on all sides
We are all connected
We can never be apart.

Heaven

I think Heaven
is exactly what you wish it to be

I mean
if it's something you don't like
then it can't be Heaven!
How could you get to Heaven
and be disappointed?

Think of how delicious some foods are
and how we take a bite
of our favorite dish and say
"This is Heaven!"
For me that might be chicken fettuccine.
For you it might be sushi.
But if you take me to
the best sushi restaurant you know
I definitely won't feel like I'm in heaven.
I guess Heaven must be subjective.

I believe Heaven is what is
most beautiful
and joyful
and exciting
and delicious
to each one of us.

It is a state of bliss
though bliss is different
for each of us.

I don't know how that works.
It just makes sense to me.

Mothers

Mother I am
Heart from my heart
Flesh from my flesh
Breath from my breath
Precious jewels
Deepest love
Eternal bond

Mother I have
Ever watchful
Ever present
No words needed
Two minds as one
Thoughts intertwined
Forever love

Mother Divine
Reaching
From you to me
And me to you
Connecting two worlds
Ever present
Unwavering grace

We are eternally
Maternally
Linked.

Remember

We are here to remember
Who we *are*

And in each moment
To create anew
Who we wish to *be*

We are here to follow our hearts
And find our bliss
Because in our hearts
And in that bliss

Is truth

And in that truth is
Who we are

Ah…
I see…

It is a circle
Never ending

We create it all
If you are looking for Heaven
Then find it
Follow it
It is there within
Your deepest self

Great

Near the flickering flame
of a candle
my hand is guided
to move
to express my soul
a conduit
through which love flows
through which truth flows
the candle's flickering flame
enlightens me.

A question:
so often I feel the desire
to do great things,
but what is "great?"
Define it:

Great
is that from which love flows,
not that which draws
admiration from the masses,
but the touching
of even one heart,

one heart...

connection
love

joy
peace;

that
is great.

Unlayering

Some of us,
for most of our lives,
have been wrapped in clothes
of falsehood.
Some of the clothes came from school.
Some came from our churches.
Some were given to us by people around us,
maybe even family.

We continue to wear the clothes
of falsity
until
one day
they just no longer fit.
They become uncomfortable
and we know
we can no longer wear them.

And so
we begin to remove them
one piece at a time.
We begin to throw them out.
We soon empty the closets
creating space for
Truth to show itself.

Some people protest,
trying to put us down,

and shaming us into wearing
the same clothes again.
But we know that once the truth
starts coming through,
there is no turning back.

And after the clothes
of fallacy
have been removed,
we see ourselves—
our authentic selves—
for the very first time.
We cry tears of relief.
We feel an inner joy,
a peace
that surpasses all understanding.

And we know,
we *know,*
that all is right and good,
as the light of our genuine selves
can now shine brightly,
unhindered by pretense,
expressing Divine Love.

Alignment

Guide me

help me to discern

that which is most important

in alignment with the path

I walk here

on this Earth.

Within

There is already
Within me
A book
An artwork
A musical composition
A dance.

There is no need
To reach outside of myself for it
It is there
It exists.

By simply being
My True Self
I can uncover
That book
That artwork
That musical composition
That dance.

Ah, there's the rub
The noise of expectations
That often swirl around me
Making it difficult
For me to find
Me.

Let go of the empty notions

That the outside world
Wraps me into.

My authentic light
Will effortlessly
Expose the gifts.

They are already in me.

Mosaic

All falls into place
A puzzle
A mosaic

Brightly colored cut pieces
When separate
Are not nearly as magnificent
As when all are in place

No need to try

Trust
Breathe
Play
And fly

Keep it simple, my dear
You tend to complicate it
And then it is burdensome
Too heavy and it cannot fly

It will take flight
If you let go.

Lenses

It is the same God
That we can view
With different lenses
Lenses of various cultures
And faiths
It is the same Spirit.

Wear the lens that feels
Most comfortable to you
And from time to time
When it feels right
Change the lens
And enjoy the feel
The view
From another perspective.

Conduit

Your fingers grip
And feel the pen
Electricity flows through

That is the energy
The energy of you
Flowing
Connecting
Embracing
Feeling the oneness
The unity

Nothing is lost
All is here
Still here, my dear
Allow, allow
Feel the grace
The gift
It is yours to bask in
And to give
To share

All love
All connection
No fear
On the right track

An expression
Of truth.

Reflection

The only sin
Is in not loving yourself.
This is the source
Of our pain.

For once you
Remember who you are—
Which is Love—
You will then be able
To see this truth in others,
This Divine DNA,
And you will love them too.

Breathe In, Breathe Out

In meditation I received…

Hold tight
Hold up
We are here
It may not always be apparent

Check in with your heart
Breathe in
Breathe out
We are that close
Know
Believe
Endless love
Endless connection

Grace…
It is even greater
Than you can imagine
Touch…
Dip your hand
Into the waters of truth
Float with us

You cannot fall
You are eternally supported
By love
A kiss
A star
Always held
Always loved.

A Taste

Castles—yes!
A lofty idea
You will enjoy this in Heaven
Piercing sapphire skies
Overlooking wildflowers
And fields of green.

Cakes—yes!
If you please
Cherries and chocolates
With mounds of sweetness
Delectable and delightful
All awaits you in Heaven.

And when you enjoy them here—
It is a taste of that divine space.

For Heaven is sprinkled all over
The Earth
To remind you
Of its existence
To help you through
The challenging times
To help you along the way
As you continue your journey here
Until it is your time
To come home.
Until then

The ineffable moments
The inexpressible beauty
The indescribable joys
Are all around.

This Blessed Moment

I am here
Just here
Just me
No more
No less
Than anyone else.

I show up
I breathe in
I breathe out
I move about
In this space
I do not wish to try
To force anything
I look around
I listen

Guide me
Please
I will follow in the footsteps
You illuminate for me
Along the way

As I step
There will be

No bells or whistles
For those are just
A loud clanging

There will only be
The softness of my steps
Upon the brilliance
Of divine guidance
Only the feeling
The knowing
That my steps are steady
They are gentle

All I can offer is me
Right here
Right now
In this blessed moment.

That Slice of Pie

The privilege of the dawn
Complete stillness
A journey
Of vanilla and pink
Plum and pomegranate
Crimson blush

Somewhere in distant lands
There is marching
There is unrest
There is hate
My mind knows it

My heart says,
"Fear not
You are here, right here
With the darting finches
Propelled by joy
Absorb this
Know this
Here and now"

In this moment
Where time stands still
I find that peace
That slice of pie
That heaven
And send it out

To the world

You are here, my God
I am your student
Here and now
In the stillness.

Revealed

How beautiful
The rediscovery
The remembering
Of who I really am
My self
My truth

It got covered up
By the shoulds and the shouldn'ts
The comparisons
And the measurements

I lost sight of it
As I tried to be
What others thought
I should be

No more

I peel away the falsehoods
Tightly wrapped around
My light
Not easy

But once I got started
I could not let it lapse
My truth
My wholeness

Revealed
Little by little
A breath of fresh air

There you are
I've missed you

Show me the way.

Detour

There are many detours
On the path of life
Sometimes—
Or even often—
You discover something
You never saw before
Never knew
Never noticed
Something you wouldn't have found
If you had not taken
The detour.

Awakening

It is a gradual process
Awakening
Gradual like the rising sun
Each moment is unique
Each moment is the right moment
For that moment
Each moment is savored
Filled with an anticipatory quality
That is cherished
Not overlooked
Not underestimated
But foundational
To the next moment
That today I see
The fullness
Of each moment
The value
The promise
The joy
The presence
Of Spirit.

Do You Call Me by Name?

Do you call me by name?
Do I hear you?

Stars surround me.
Your peace and your presence
Flowing through me.
May I stay this way forever?

Through each day
And each moment
As I look into the eyes
Of those around me,
All the others,
As beloved to you
As I am to you
And you are to me,
The softness
Of true love and peace,
The Holy Spirit
Flows through me
Through us
For we are all connected.

But do we see the flame
Resting above our heads?
That is the aura
The awareness
Of Grace

Of Spirit.

And the white dove…
May I see the white dove
As a sign
A symbol
Of your ever-present love.

The Path

Clear the path
As I walk upon it.
Clear it of debris
That may get in the way.
Any obstacles,
Any hindrances,
For the path takes me to Truth,
To Love,
To Heaven.

Clear the path
So that I may have the ability
To follow it in its purity.
Guide me so I may not lose my footing.
And as I walk along,
Let us dance,
Let us reach and sing,
For we cannot contain our joy.

All the paths around me
At times converge.
Our paths are individual
As our fingerprints,
And yet,
We often see the convergence
Of one upon the other,
Intersecting,
Bonding,

Absorbing,
Then releasing,
Expressing individuality again,
Then merging again.

A flow,
A glow,
A luminescence
Of lighted paths.
A light show,
Beautiful beyond imagination,
Of truth,
Of clarity,
Of divinity.

Are You Listening?

Are you listening to yourself?

Deep within,
Where God resides—
That is the sound
Of perfect peace.
Your true self,
Who you came here to be.
That is where you find resonance.

When you go to that place,
You can release the noise of the world,
All the distractions,
And instead listen to
Your own voice
Intertwined with God's.
You will find yourself.
You will find Truth.

Retreat
Within
To the safety of your true self,
Not the outer self
That compares itself
To others in this world.
The inner self knows
There is no comparison,
For you are

Uniquely you
And that is enough,
That is precious,
That is your gift
To the world.

Are you listening?

A Bird Called Wisdom

In the dream
I stood in a space
Nondescript
It was warm
It was safe
A bird flew to me
And hovered right in front of my face
He was young, meek, peaceful
I reached out
And held his sweet body in my hands
I had always wanted to hold a bird like this
I was thrilled to hold him so close.

As we silently smiled at each other
In a space where nothing else mattered
Another bird flew over
She was a bit older
Confident and knowledgeable
And hovered in the air
As I continued to hold Little Bird
The older bird spoke to me
And we had a conversation
Of a spiritual nature
Though I do not recall the words
There was no doubt about
The sincerity
And grace
Of this experience

Suspended in timelessness.

She soon indicated
That it was time for the two of them to go
I knew it was alright
And I would be fine
But as they were about to leave
I blurted, "Wait! What is your name?"
She looked at me and cooed,
"Wisdom,"
Then flew away.

Strange Paradox

There is a strange paradox
So much pain
So much grief
So much devastation
So much tragedy
So much loss
So much confusion

All of it flows
Somehow
With grace
To a very beautiful place

A place of caring
A place of love and support
A place of expression
A place of memories
A place of illumination
A place of beauty
And ultimately
A place of joy

A place I never would have known
With the same depth
Had I not experienced
The pain

It is a paradox

It is an unexpected gift.

I Didn't Think

I didn't think I could survive
But I did

I didn't want to keep living
But now I do

Because I know
You are by my side

And I've got a lot of
Living and loving
Still to do
As I honor you
My son
My Eric
For the rest of my Earthly days.

Peace

About the Author

Dolores Cruz began writing professionally after the unexpected passing away of her youngest son, Eric. Her book, *A Bird Named Wisdom*, is a collection of poems taken from her journals written during the first 6 years after her son's transition to spirit. Cruz's first book, *Look Around; A Mother's Journey from Grief and Despair to Healing and Hope,* chronicles her life before, during, and after Eric's accident.

Dolores continues to honor Eric by sharing healing and hope with other parents whose children have passed away by volunteering with grief support groups. Her family also provides a scholarship for drum students at a nearby music school.

Dolores is a retired schoolteacher who enjoys reading and yoga, and teaches tap dance through the local community college. You can read more of Dolores's writings by visiting her blog at doloreslookaround.blogspot.com. and learn more about her through her website, doloreslookaround.com.

Dolores resides near Los Angeles, California with her husband, Joey, and boxer dog, Brandy.

Printed in Great Britain
by Amazon

34186426R00138